Bond Assessment Papers

Fifth papers in English

J M Bond and Sarah Lindsay

Key words

Some special words are used in this book. You will find them picked out in **bold** in the Papers. These words are explained here.

abbreviation	a word or words which is/are shortened
adjective	a word that describes somebody or something
adverb	a word that gives extra meaning to a verb
alphabetical order	words arranged in the order found in the alphabet
antonym	a word with a meaning opposite to another word *hot – cold*
clause	a section of a sentence with a verb
compound word	a word made up of two other words *football*
conditional	a clause or sentence expressing the idea that one thing depends on something else
conjunction	a word used to link sentences, phrases or words *and, but*
connective	a word or words that joins clauses or sentences
contraction	two words shortened into one with an apostrophe placed where the letter/s have been dropped *do not = don't*
definition	meanings of words
diminutive	a word implying smallness *booklet*
homophone	a word that has the same sound as another but a different meaning or spelling *right / write*
infinitive	the base form of a verb without any additional endings *clap*
metaphor	a figurative expression in which something is described in terms usually associated with another *the sky is a sapphire sea*
mnemonic	a device to learn particular spellings *There is a rat in separate.*
noun	a word for somebody or something
collective noun	a word referring to a group *swarm*
onomatopoeic	a word that echoes a sound, associated with its meaning *hiss*
past tense	something that has already happened
phrase	a group of words that act as a unit
adjectival phrase	a group of words describing a noun
plural	more than one *cats*
prefix	a group of letters added to the beginning of a word *un, dis*
preposition	a word that relates other words to each other *the book on the table*
pronoun	a word used to replace a noun *them*
root word	a word to which prefixes or suffixes can be added to make other words *quickly*
sentence	a unit of written language which makes sense by itself
active	when the main person or thing does the action *he took it*
passive	when the main person or thing has the action done to it *it was taken by him*
simile	an expression to describe what something is like *as cold as ice*
singular	one *cat*
suffix	a group of letters added to the end of a word *ly, ful*
superlative	describes the limit of a quality (adjective or adverb) *most/least or shortest*
synonym	a word with the same or very similar meaning as another word *quick – fast*
verb	a 'doing' or 'being' word

Paper 1

The weather was exceptionally mild that Christmas holiday and one amazing morning our whole family got ready to go for our first drive in the first motor-car we had ever owned. This new motor-car was an enormous long black French automobile called a De Dion-Bouton which had a canvas roof that folded back. The driver was to be that twelve-years-older-than-me half-sister (now aged twenty-one) who had recently had her appendix removed.

She had received two full half-hour lessons in driving from the man who delivered the car, and in that enlightened year of 1925 this was considered quite sufficient. Nobody had to take a driving-test. You were your own judge of competence, and as soon as you felt you were ready to go, off you jolly well went.

As we all climbed into the car, our excitement was so intense we could hardly bear it.

'How fast will it go?' we cried out. 'Will it do fifty miles an hour?'

'It'll do sixty!' the ancient sister answered. Her tone was so confident and cocky it should have scared us to death, but it didn't.

'Oh, let's make it do sixty!' we shouted. 'Will you promise to take us up to sixty?'

'We shall probably go faster than that,' the sister announced, pulling on her driving-gloves and tying a scarf over her head in the approved driving-fashion of the period.

The canvas hood had been folded back because of the mild weather, converting the car into a magnificent open tourer. Up front, there were three bodies in all, the driver behind the wheel, my half-brother (aged eighteen) and one of my sisters (aged twelve). In the back seat there were four more of us, my mother (aged forty), two small sisters (aged eight and five) and myself (aged nine). Our machine possessed one very special feature which I don't think you see on the cars of today. This was a second windscreen in the back solely to keep the breeze off the faces of the back-seat passengers when the hood was down. It had a long centre section and two little end sections that could be angled backwards to deflect the wind.

From *Boy* by Roald Dahl

Underline the correct answers.

1   In which year did Roald Dahl have his first drive in a car?
    (1952, 1825, <u>1925</u>)

2   Where was the car made?
    (England, <u>France</u>, Germany)

3   How many passengers travelled in the car on Roald Dahl's first trip?
    (3, 4, <u>7</u>)

Answer these questions.

4 How fast did the passengers want to travel?

The passengers wanted to travel 60 miles a hour

5 What was a feature of this car that is not found on cars today?

_____

6 Why do you think Roald Dahl called his sister 'ancient'?

_____

7 Describe how you think the passengers were feeling.

_____

_____

8 Which line indicates that Roald Dahl's sister might not be a very good driver even though she thought she was?

_____

_____

9–10 Write down two events that might have occurred during Roald Dahl's first journey in a car.

_____

_____

7

Form a **noun** from each of the **verbs** in bold.

11 **provide**   They bought the _____ at the supermarket.

12 **enter**   They couldn't find the _____ to the caves.

13 **choose**   They had the _____ of going to the seaside or to a farm.

14 **advertise**   The _____ said that the concert started at 7.30 p.m.

15 **perform**   The _____ of the school play was excellent.

16 **bewilder**   The child's _____ was plain to see.

17 **destroy**   The army was responsible for the _____ of the bridge.

18 **applaud**   The _____ was deafening.

8

Fill in the missing letter in each word with an *a*, *e* or *o*.

19 decorat___r   20 cell___r   21 plumb___r

22 disast___r   23 corrid___r   24 burgl___r

25 popul___r   26 circul___r   27 divis___r

28 direct___r   29 propriet___r   30 partn___r

`12`

Write the following using indirect speech.

31–35 Dad said, "I am going to mow the lawn. I hope this is the last time I will have to do it this year as I am tired of doing it."

Dad said that _____ going to mow the lawn.

_____ this _____ the last time _____

have to do it this year as _____ tired of doing it.

`5`

Put these words in **alphabetical order**.

schooner   scheme   scholar   school   sceptre

36 (1) _____   **37** (2) _____   **38** (3) _____

39 (4) _____   **40** (5) _____

`5`

Write *there*, *their* or *they're* in each gap.

41–42 _____ going to dive into the pool when _____ teacher blows the whistle.

43–44 Where are _____ coats? _____ soaking!

45–46 _____ is no point hiding the chocolate box _____ !

47–48 _____ is a strong wind which has blown some tiles off _____ roof.

`8`

Write the **contraction** for each of these.

49 should not _____   **50** they will _____

51 there will _____   **52** had not _____

53 there is _____   **54** they have _____

55 I would _____   **56** will not _____

`8`

In each space, write the word class of the word in bold.

57 Close the **back** door. _____

58 We said we would **back** Hotspot to win the race. _____

59 Dad's got a pain in his **back**. _____

60 Come **back** soon. _____

4

Write three **compound words** using each of the words listed.

61–63 light _____ _____ _____

64–66 snow _____ _____ _____

67–69 day _____ _____ _____

9

Underline the unstressed vowels in each word.

70 postage   **71** sentence   **72** parliament

73 machinery   **74** fattening   **75** mathematics

76 history

7

Rewrite these sentences changing them from **singular** to **plural**.

77–80 The man was cleaning his house.

_____

81–82 She jumped over the puddle.

_____

83–86 He bought a scarf to support his football team.

_____

10

Match a word from the box to complete each proverb.

work	lining	thoughts	speed
never	thorns	news	water	basket

87 A penny for your _____ .

88 A rose between two _____ .

89 Better late than _____ .

90 Blood is thicker than _____ .

91 Many hands make light _____ .

92 Every cloud has a silver _____ .

93 Don't put all your eggs in one _____ .

94 No news is good _____ .

95 More haste, less _____ .

Rewrite the passage adding the missing commas.

96–100 Sam was caught thank goodness otherwise I would have been blamed for stealing the sweets pen magazine Harry Potter book and racing car.

_____

_____

_____

_____

Paper 2

WHAT IS THE PARANORMAL?

The word 'paranormal' simply means 'beyond normal'. It suggests that there are two categories of event – some that are normal, and some that are not. This categorisation is based on our belief that things can't be normal if science doesn't have an explanation for them.

Paranormal activities

'The paranormal' is a general term for all paranormal subjects or happenings. These range from spoon bending to UFO sightings and spooky hauntings. The four most well-documented areas are poltergeists, extra-sensory perception, ghosts, and aliens.

Poltergeists and ghosts

Poltergeists show themselves by what they do, for example making noises or moving

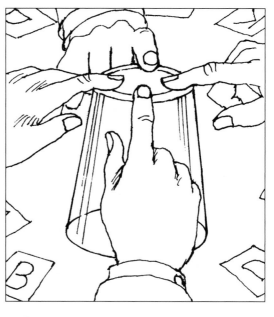

'Extra' is another way of saying beyond, so ESP means experiences we couldn't have had via our sight, smell, hearing, taste or touch. Most scientists believe we learn all we know through our senses, but if ESP exists, we may learn things in other, more mysterious ways.

Aliens
Most people think of aliens as beings from outer space who visit our planet in Unidentified Flying Objects, or UFOs. If you see a UFO, it's called a close encounter of the first kind. If a UFO leaves a mark, like a burn on the ground, it is an encounter of the second kind. In an encounter of the third kind, you actually meet aliens. The fourth kind is alien abduction.

things around. They are often thought of as a type of ghost, but they are usually invisible. Ghosts are generally visions or apparitions – in other words, people can see them. Victims of either poltergeists or ghosts are referred to as 'haunted'. Dishes being thrown or smashed is a common sign of poltergeist activity.

Extra-sensory perception
Extra-sensory perception is often shortened to ESP.

From *The Usborne Book of the Paranormal*

Underline the correct answers.

1   What is a common sign of poltergeist activity?
    (an image moving across a room, a dish being thrown, a UFO landing)

2   If you know something by ESP, can you can see it?
    (yes, no, sometimes)

3   What is an encounter of the third kind?
    (an alien abduction, a UFO seen in the sky, meeting an alien)

3

Answer these questions.

4   Explain what the word 'paranormal' means.

    _____

5   What definition is used to describe whether things are 'normal' or not?

    _____

6   When is a person referred to as 'haunted'?

    _____

7   Which area of paranormal activities do you find most interesting? Why?

    _____

    _____

8–9 Describe a difference in the ways you might react to being aware of a poltergeist and an encounter of the third kind.

_____

_____

_____

6

Give the **plurals** of the following **nouns**.

10	mouse	_____	**11**	story	_____
12	cargo	_____	**13**	thief	_____
14	trolley	_____	**15**	potato	_____
16	gas	_____	**17**	ox	_____
18	roof	_____	**19**	valley	_____

10

Match the words with their definitions. Write the correct number in the space.

20	conflagration	_____	(1)	secret
21	conservation	_____	(2)	assembly
22	constellation	_____	(3)	disastrous fire
23	conversation	_____	(4)	group of stars
24	confidential	_____	(5)	one after the other, in order
25	consecutive	_____	(6)	preservation
26	congregation	_____	(7)	informal discussion

7

Put the words in bold in their correct places so the extract below makes sense.

27–36   **movement**   **wedge**   **cook**   **ashore**   **crutch**

deck   **walk**   **spaces**   **lanyard**   **heaviest**

Long John Silver, our ship's _____ – Barbecue as the men called him –

carried his _____ by a _____ round his neck, to have both hands as

free as possible. It was something to see him _____ the foot of his

crutch against a bulkhead, and, propped against it, yielding to every

_____ of the ship, get on with his cooking like someone safe _____.

9

Still more strange was it to see him in the _____ of weather, cross the

_____ . He had a line or two rigged up to help him across the widest

_____ and he would hand himself from one place to another as quickly

as another man could _____ .

10

Complete the following **similes** using the words in the box.

two peas	pie	hatter	cucumber
lead	bat	cricket	gold

37 as alike as _____

38 as blind as a _____

39 as cool as a _____

40 as easy as _____

41 as good as _____

42 as heavy as _____

43 as lively as a _____

44 as mad as a _____

8

Underline the **verbs** in the sentences.

45 She walked slowly to school today.

46 Ian had a large appetite.

47 Rachel wrote the invitations to her party neatly.

48 She intently watched the TV programme.

49 Softly she sang the lilting tune.

50 They got up early on Sunday.

51–52 He lifted the kitten carefully and put it in the basket.

8

Write an **antonym** for each of these words.

53 contract _____

54 import _____

55 increase _____

56 fine _____

57 captive _____

58 temporary _____

59 superior _____

60 refuse _____

61 plural _____

62 destroy _____

10

Rewrite the statements as questions and the questions as statements.

63 Jess loves going swimming.

_____

64 Does Alice enjoy painting?

_____

65 Is Bola's coat in the car?

_____

66 Daniel has dropped his homework without noticing.

_____

67 Have they all received an invitation from Amita?

_____

68 Ruben has eaten the last cake.

_____

6

Fill the gap by writing the **past tense** of the word in bold.

69 **creep** They _____ slowly towards her.

70 **lose** He _____ his ball when he was out in the woods.

71 **speak** The lady _____ kindly to the little girl.

72 **weep** Sam _____ when the kitten died.

73 **throw** Ian _____ the ball over the wall.

74 **ring** The policewoman _____ the doorbell.

75 **write** They _____ long stories.

76 **break** Mum was cross when they _____ the plate.

8

Circle the **pronouns** in the short passage.

77–83 They jumped into the car before it sped off at high speed. Joseph whispered that he had never seen his mum so cross. She reminded him of a bull! They agreed with him.

7

Copy and add the missing punctuation to the following:

84–88 What about the horse said Thorin You don't mention sending that back

_____

_____

_____

5

Write three words with each of the **prefixes**.

89–91 **dis-** _____   _____   _____

92–94 **mis-** _____   _____   _____

6

Write interesting sentences, including an **adjective** and an **adverb** in each, using the nouns and verbs provided.

95–96 daughter   enquire

_____

97–98 chocolate   climb

_____

99–100 people   react

_____

6

100 TOTAL

Paper 3

Stopping by Woods on a Snowy Evening

Whose woods these are I think I know.
His house is in the village, though;
He will not see me stopping here
To watch his woods fill up with snow.

My little horse must think it queer
To stop without a farmhouse near
Between the woods and frozen lake
The darkest evening of the year.

He gives his harness bells a shake
To ask if there is some mistake.
The only other sound's the sweep
Of easy wind and downy flake.

The woods are lovely, dark, and deep,
But I have promises to keep,
And miles to go before I sleep,
And miles to go before I sleep.

by Robert Frost

Underline the correct answers.

1   At what time of day is this poem set?
     (morning, afternoon, evening)

2   Where does the owner of the woods live?
     (in a farmhouse, in the woods, in a village)

3   Where does the rider stop his horse?
     (in the woods, beside the woods, a long way from the woods)

Answer these questions.

4–5   Describe two sounds the rider can hear.

_____

_____

6   Why would the rider's horse think it 'queer' to stop where they have?

_____

7   Which line in the poem highlights the fact the rider loves the woods, rather than
     is frightened of them?

_____

8   How do you think you would feel about the woods if you were making the same
     journey? Why?

_____

_____

9   Why do you think the final two lines of the poem have been repeated?

_____

_____

Underline the words below which are of common gender.

10–16   actress   athlete   student   widow

             policeman   friend   dustman   typist

             knitter   bride   bachelor   mother

             girl   child   cat   businessman

Write the following **abbreviations** in full.

17 NE _____

18 PLC _____

19 PTO _____

20 Dept _____

21 mg _____

22 MP _____

23 BST _____

24 UK _____

Complete each expression with a **preposition**.

Example   *off* the cuff

25 _____ the most part   26 _____ the long run

27 _____ all fours   28 _____ the other hand

29 _____ better or worse   30 _____ his wits' end

31 _____ all means   32 _____ to the hilt

Complete the following words with *ie* or *ei*.

33 for_____gn   34 bel_____ve   35 ach_____ve

36 conc_____ted   37 n_____ghbour   38 aud_____nce

39 h_____ght   40 c_____ling

On each line, underline the word which is the same part of speech as the word in bold.

41	**often**	noble	beautiful	sick	badly	wanting
42	**breathe**	quickly	goat	it	for	slither
43	**height**	quantity	sit	idle	lazy	comfortable
44	**difficult**	soften	woollen	they	worm	grew
45	**why**	time	place	where	town	hour
46	**sad**	dress	bonnet	ship	picture	ugly
47	**and**	sand	boat	badly	but	cut

Complete the second **clause** for each of these sentences.

48 I went to a swimming party but _____

_____

49 The fierce dog chased Euan until _____

_____

50 The autumn leaves spun in the wind while _____

_____

51 Kitty spoke sternly to her friend because _____

_____

52 Tuhil didn't appreciate the consequence of his actions until _____

_____

53 Our teacher was rushed to hospital after _____

_____

6

Write two words that use the **root word** in bold.

54–55 **help**   _____   _____

56–57 **turn**   _____   _____

58–59 **collect**   _____   _____

60–61 **reason**   _____   _____

62–63 **agree**   _____   _____

10

Underline any of these words which should always start with a capital letter.

64–72

envelope	egyptian	film	david	february
wales	food	function	denmark	nation
month	june	manchester	ornament	tuesday
queen	kite	britney	log	lion

9

15

Write two definitions for each of these words. One might be a meaning that has evolved over recent years.

73–74 wicked

(1) _____

(2) _____

75–76 trainer

(1) _____

(2) _____

77–78 cool

(1) _____

(2) _____

79–80 green

(1) _____

(2) _____

8

Make **nouns** from the words in bold to complete the sentences.

81 punish   I do not believe in capital _____.

82 fragrant The _____ of the rose was beautiful.

83 arrive   The _____ of the pop star at the airport was delayed.

84 long   Sarah said that her trousers were not the right _____.

85 conclude At the _____ of the concert we rushed to get home.

86 assist   Dad asked Najib for his _____.

6

Rewrite these sentences so they contain only single negatives.

87 Gina didn't swim in no sea.

_____

88 There weren't no stars out tonight.

_____

89 The dogs didn't not wait.

_____

90 The playground wasn't not open.

_____

91 Caroline didn't want no ride in the car.

_____

92 Raj's family hadn't won no money on the lottery.

_____

6

Write eight **contractions** using the words in bold.

| are | you | have | will | they | not |

93–100 _____ _____ _____ _____

_____ _____ _____ _____

8

100
TOTAL

Paper 4

WEATHERING THE STORM

Britain's nature reserves – the human insurance policy to provide havens to keep rare species alive – are threatened as climate change begins to bite. Static chunks of land are changing character, and different weather patterns and sea level rise threaten to wash some away altogether. Plants, animals and birds must move or be moved to survive.

For the Royal Society for the Protection of Birds (RSPB), with 170 reserves covering more than 280,000 acres, this is already a problem. Titchwell, one of its most popular reserves, 21 miles from King's Lynn in Norfolk, and the home of the RSPB's emblem – the avocet – is more frequently being inundated by the sea. The problem of sea level rise, caused by global warming, is made worse by increased storminess.

The society believes it will be hard to protect all the freshwater habitats on the reserve for more than a decade or two. Already these are artificially maintained to some extent, by pumping water around.

There are other problems inland. The Ouse Washes, in Cambridgeshire and Lincolnshire, managed for breeding waders, is also increasingly flooded to the extent that much of it is often no longer suitable habitat for the birds. So the RSPB are looking to acquire less flood-prone land alongside the Washes. But there are similar problems elsewhere.

A host of scientific evidence indicates that wild plants and animals have responded to the climate change that has already occurred. Migratory birds arrive earlier, nest earlier, and leave later.

Butterflies have moved their ranges northwards or upwards in altitude. On average, trees across Europe come into leaf six days earlier than they did 20 years ago and leaf fall is four days later. Little egrets now come to southern England from France, and the Dartford warbler is heading north.

Such trends are likely to continue, with wild species trying to extend their ranges northwards or to higher altitudes to match the changing climate. But some species will be unable to move. For them, the prospect of extinction looms.

From _The Guardian Society_ Wednesday, October 3, 2001

Underline the correct answers.

1 How many nature reserves does the RSPB have?
(21, 170, 280)

2 What is the RSPB's emblem?
(the avocet, the sea, the wader)

Answer these questions.

3 Why are Britain's nature reserves so important?

_____

_____

4 What is threatening Britain's nature reserves?

_____

_____

5–6 List two specific problems mentioned in the article that are affecting the RSPB's reserves.

_____

_____

_____

7 What is likely to happen to many birds, insects and plants that are unable to move from the habitats they are now in?

_____

_____

8–9 Humans can help in the relocation of species. List two considerations that you think might need to be made when humans become involved.

_____

_____

_____

_____

Write three **onomatopoeic** words that describe sounds made by the following:

10–12 an engine _____ _____ _____

13–15 the wind _____ _____ _____

16–18 water _____ _____ _____

9

Add the **suffix** *ing* to each of the following words. Rewrite the words correctly.

19 put _____ **20** talk _____ **21** do _____

22 swim _____ **23** use _____ **24** hide _____

25 hope _____ **26** get _____ **27** carry _____

9

Add a **conjunction** to each sentence.

28 Mum got tea ready _____ I did my homework.

29 We wanted to play tennis _____ there were no courts available.

30 Our class went to Higham Castle _____ we saw a ducking stool.

31 You cannot watch TV _____ you have tidied your bedroom.

32 You must eat fish _____ it is good for you.

33 We know you broke the window _____ we saw you do it.

34 They were crossing the road _____ we saw them.

7

The following words end in either *ent* or *ant*. Add the correct ending to each word.

35 eleg_____ **36** prud_____ **37** adjac_____

38 abund_____ **39** arrog_____ **40** extravag_____

41 contin_____ **42** immigr_____ **43** cem_____

9

Rewrite the phrases below in more formal English.

44 See ya later.

_____

45 You're taking the mickey!

_____

46 I ain't having none of that.

_____

47 Did you wag school?

_____

48 It was an awesome gig.

_____

49 Be there or be square.

_____

50 You look cool in those sun glasses.

_____

7

Add the missing colons.

51 The following children are absent today Amina, Ilesh, Frank, Michael and Fayza.

52 The school magazine reported No school uniform for a day!

53 An eyewitness stated The car turned over as it crashed into the tree, just missing three people ...

54 The following classes are out on a school trip today Class 6L, Class 6T and Class 6M.

55 The local paper reported School flooded, children sent home.

5

Circle the **diminutives**.

56–62

golden	piglet	classroom	penknife
statuette	droplet	daylight	owlet
duckling	starlet	appearance	majorette

7

Write the possessive form of each of the following.

63 food for the rabbit

_____

64 hairbrush for Leanne

_____

65 football for the players

_____

66 rattle for the baby

_____

67 cafe for the museum

_____

68 playground for toddlers _____

69 handlebar of a bicycle _____

70 newspaper for Mr Dodd _____

Improve these sentences by changing the group of words in bold for a single one.

71 The children were delighted to be able to talk to the **person who wrote the book**. _____

72 The teacher put the **pens, rulers, pencils and rubbers** in the cupboard. _____

73 Peter **said he was sorry** for what he had done. _____

74 The weather has improved **during the last day or two**. _____

75 The children who were **at school that day** put up the decorations. _____

76 Gareth thought it **a waste of time** to copy the words of the song when he could already sing it perfectly. _____

Write words with the following number of syllables.

77 2 syllables _____

78–79 3 syllables _____ _____

80–81 4 syllables _____ _____

82–83 5 syllables _____ _____

84–85 6 syllables _____ _____

Rewrite the passage, adding the missing punctuation. Start new lines where necessary.

86–100 I will buy you some new shoes said Mum but not until you have out-grown the ones you are wearing now But these aren't fashionable complained Sam Nobody has shoes like these now You do laughed Mum

_____

_____

_____

_____

_____

15

100
TOTAL

Paper 5

We judged that three more nights would fetch us to Cairo, at the bottom of Illinois, where the Ohio River comes in, and that was what we was after. We would sell the raft and get on a steamboat and go way up the Ohio amongst the free States, and then be out of trouble.

Well, the second night a fog begun to come on, and we made for a tow-head to tie to, for it wouldn't do to try to run in fog; but when I paddled ahead in the canoe, with the line, to make fast, there warn't anything but little saplings to tie to. I passed the line around one of them right on the edge of the cut bank, but there was a stiff current, and the raft come booming down so lively she tore it out by but the roots and away she went. I see the fog closing down, and it made me so sick and scared I couldn't budge for most a half a minute it seemed to me – and then there warn't no raft in sight; you couldn't see twenty yards. I jumped into the canoe and run back to the stem and grabbed the paddle and set her back a stroke. But she didn't come. I was in such a hurry I hadn't untied her. I got up and tried to untie her, but I was so excited my hands shook so I couldn't hardly do anything with them.

As soon as I got started I took out after the raft, hot and heavy, right down the tow-head. That was all right as far as it went, but the tow-head warn't sixty yards long, and the minute I flew by the foot of it I shot out into the solid white fog, and hadn't no more idea which way I was going than a dead man.

Thinks I, it won't do to paddle; first I know I'll run into the bank or a tow-head or something; I got to set still and float, and yet it's mighty fidgety business to have to hold your hands still at such a time. I whooped and listened. Away down there, somewheres, I hear a small whoop, and up comes my spirits. I went tearing after it, listening sharp to hear it again. The next time it come, I see I warn't heading for it but heading away to the right of it. And the next time, I was heading away to the left of it – and not gaining on it much, either, for I was flying around, this way and that and t'other, but it was going straight ahead all the time.

I did wish the fool would think to beat a tin pan, and beat it all the time, but he never did, and it was the still places between the whoops that was making the trouble for me. Well, I fought along, and directly I hears the whoop *behind* me. I was tangled good, now. That was somebody else's whoop, or else I was turned around.

I throwed the paddle down. I heard the whoop again; it was behind me yet, but in a different place; it kept coming, and kept changing its place, and I kept answering, till by-and-by it was in front of me again and I knowed the current had swung the canoe's head down-stream and I was all right, if that was Jim and not some other raftsman hollering. I couldn't tell nothing about voices in a fog, for nothing don't look natural nor sound natural in a fog.

From *The Adventures of Huckleberry Finn* by Mark Twain

Underline the correct answers.

1   Where was the narrator, Huckleberry Finn, heading on the raft?
    (Ohio, Connecticut, Cairo)

2   Was Huckleberry Finn travelling alone?
    (Yes, No)

3   On which night did the fog descend?
    (first, second, third)

3

Answer these questions.

4   Write the phrase from the passage that helps us appreciate how thick the fog was.

    _____

5–6   Huckleberry Finn felt 'scared' and 'excited' in this passage.

    Describe why you think he felt each of these emotions.

    scared   _____

    excited _____

7   Why was Huckleberry Finn travelling at night?

    _____

    _____

8   Find a word in the passage that means 'shouting' or 'shouted'.

    _____

9   Why do you think 'nothing don't look natural nor sound natural in a fog'?

    _____

6

To each **verb** add an **adverb** that could describe it.

10   spent   _____   11   ate   _____

12   shone   _____   13   remembered _____

14 listened   _____   **15** wrote   _____

16 fought   _____   **17** helped   _____

WEST END SHOW

seeks

attractive

DOG

(either sex)

OPEN AUDITION ON-STAGE

12 Noon Monday May 12

ESSENTIAL to all applicants:

NO stage-fright.
Good sense of rhythm.

Clean grooming an advantage.

All enquiries ring Production Office

Tel: 020 8042 7918

18–20 List three qualities the dogs must be able to show.

_____

_____

_____

21 Where will the auditions be held?

_____

22 What should you do if you require more information?

_____

23 What is an audition?

_____

Complete each sentence with the correct **homophone**.

24–25 **new**   **knew**

Dad _____ that I had bought a _____ pen.

26–27 **course**   **coarse**

Of _____ I knew that the material was very _____.

28–29 **beach**   **beech**

The _____ tree was in a garden quite near the _____.

30–31 **practice**   **practise**

The student dentist had to _____ checking teeth before he joined the

_____ in Upton Road.

32–33 **our**   **hour**

Just as the first _____ had passed _____ team scored a goal.

`10`

Match these words with their meanings. Write the number of the correct definition by each word.

(1) a single rail track
(2) a series of sounds of the same pitch
(3) a single colour: black and white
(4) a word of one syllable
(5) design using initials of a name
(6) a speech performed by one actor
(7) one large block of stone

34 monochrome _____   35 monogram _____

36 monolith _____   37 monologue _____

38 monorail _____   39 monosyllable _____

40 monotone _____

`7`

Add a **prefix** to make each of these words into its **antonym**.

41 lock _____   42 polite _____

43 agree _____   44 capable _____

45 regular _____   46 cover _____

47 own _____   48 reliable _____

`8`

Rewrite these sentences changing them from **plural** to **singular**.

49–51 The mice lived in the old barn until the children found them.

_____

_____

52–54 The classes lined up quietly once their teachers had arrived.

_____

55–59 The satsumas were eaten quickly by the children, who then wanted some chocolates!

_____

_____

Put these words in **alphabetical order**.

refuse   refund   refute   refugee   regard   refresh

60 (1) _____   **61** (2) _____   **62** (3) _____

63 (4) _____   **64** (5) _____   **65** (6) _____

Punctuate the passage correctly.

66–75 What time are you going home said Jill to her brother I don't want to be late Ill go when you are ready replied Tim

_____

_____

_____

Add a **clause** to each of these to make a longer sentence. Use a different **connective** each time.

76–77 Zoe sprinted, just staying ahead _____

_____

78–79 Zoe sprinted, just staying ahead _____

_____

80–81 Zoe sprinted, just staying ahead _____

_____

82–83 Jack kept his eyes firmly on the ground _____

_____

84–85 Jack kept his eyes firmly on the ground _____

_____

86–87 Jack kept his eyes firmly on the ground _____

_____

| | 12 |

Write these words in their **singular** form.

88	salmon	_____	**89**	wives	_____
90	opportunities	_____	**91**	halves	_____
92	cacti	_____	**93**	solos	_____
94	canoes	_____	**95**	puppies	_____

| | 8 |

Complete each sentence as a metaphor, using each phrase in the box once only.

cotton wool	blanket	torrent of darkness
ribbon of moonlight	soft cushion	

96 The _____ of snow lay on the fields.

97 The wind was a _____.

98 The leaves were a _____ for the falling apples.

99 The _____ clouds hid the stars.

100 The road was a _____.

| | 5 |

| | 100 |
| | **TOTAL** |

27

Paper 6

The wind was a torrent of darkness among the gusty trees,
The moon was a ghostly galleon tossed upon cloudy seas,
The road was a ribbon of moonlight over the purple moor,
And the highwayman came riding –
    Riding – riding –
The highwayman came riding, up to the old inn-door.

He'd a French cocked-hat on his forehead, a bunch of lace
    at his chin,
A coat of claret velvet, and breeches of brown doe skin;
They fitted with never a wrinkle: his boots were up to the thigh!
And he rode with a jewelled tinkle,
    His pistol butts a-twinkle,
His rapier hilt a-twinkle, under the jewelled sky.

Over the cobbles he clattered and clashed in the dark inn-yard,
And he tapped with his whip on the shutters, but all was locked and barred;
He whistled a tune to the window, and who should be waiting there
But the landlord's black-eyed daughter,
    Bess, the landlord's daughter,
Plaiting a dark red love-knot into her long black hair.

And dark in the old inn-yard a stable-wicket creaked
Where Tim the ostler listened; his face was white and peaked;
His eyes were hollows of madness, his hair like mouldy hay,
But he loved the landlord's daughter,
    The landlord's red-lipped daughter;
Dumb as a dog he listened, and he heard the robber say –

'One kiss, my bonny sweetheart, I'm after a prize tonight,
But I shall be back with the yellow gold before the morning light;
Yet, if they press me sharply, and harry me through the day,
Then look for me by moonlight,
    Watch for me by moonlight,
I'll come to thee by moonlight, though hell should bar the way.'

He rose upright in the stirrups; he scarce could reach her hand,
But she loosened her hair i' the casement! His face burnt like a brand
As the black cascade of perfume came tumbling over his breast;
And he kissed its waves in the moonlight,
    (Oh, sweet black waves in the moonlight!)
Then he tugged at his rein in the moonlight, and galloped away to the west.

From *The Highwayman* by Alfred Noyes

Underline the correct answers.

1   In what period of time was this poem set?
    (day, night, either day or night)

2   What colour was the Highwayman's coat?
    (deep red, dark brown, black)

3 How many people were in love with the landlord's daughter?
(1, 2, 3)

3

Answer these questions.

4 Explain what is meant by the words 'jewelled sky'.

_____

5 Why do you think Tim was described as 'Dumb as a dog'?

_____

6 What type of prize do you think the Highwayman was after?

_____

7 The Highwayman is a narrative poem. What is a narrative poem?

_____

8–9 Imagine you are Tim. How would you have felt listening to the conversation in the inn-yard and what would you have done once the Highwayman left?

_____

_____

_____

6

Underline the word which is the same part of speech as the word in bold.

10	**laughed**	loudly	longer	ran	wild	joker
11	**magazine**	entered	cassette	he	wrote	her
12	**tiny**	bee	wasp	flew	away	large
13	**sang**	cried	loudly	nice	silently	nation
14	**loudly**	quickly	quieten	quicken	game	film
15	**they**	boys	children	she	teacher	class

6

Add the **suffix** *able* or *ful* to the words.

16 love _____   **17** use _____   **18** plenty _____

19 wonder _____   **20** value _____   **21** laugh _____

22 right _____   **23** power _____   **24** work _____

9

Some of the following pairs of words are **synonyms** and some are **antonyms**. Put them in the correct columns in the table.

25–34   vacant/empty   absence/presence   tranquil/peaceful

option/choice   seldom/often   few/many   here/there

caution/care   coarse/fine   famous/noted

Synonyms	Antonyms

10

Write four interesting sentences. Each sentence must include one noun and one verb from those below and at least one **adjective** and one **adverb**.

noun	verb
purse	climbed
gate	opened
mountain	disappear
giraffe	ran

35–36 _____

_____

37–38 _____

_____

39–40 _____

_____

41–42 _____

8

_____

Underline any word below which does not have a specifically feminine form.
       Example actor → actress   builder → no specific feminine form

43–49 visitor   hero   waiter   worker

      manager   editor   relation   widower

      adult   mayor   pupil   passenger

7

Add the missing commas to these sentences.

50–51 One morning as the sun was rising Jack crept out of the house.

52 In his hand was a small bag just large enough to carry an apple two sandwiches and a big slice of cake.

53–54 He turned looked towards the house then ran across the field.

55 Jack moved slowly worried he might be seen.

56–58 As he entered the cave his eyes adjusting to the darkness he recognised the silhouette of Aimee his young and vulnerable sister.

9

Spell these words correctly.

59 buisness _____   **60** imaginry _____

61 consience _____   **62** enviroment _____

63 miscelaneous _____   **64** persasion _____

65 stomache _____   **66** necesary _____

67 possesion _____   **68** seqence _____

10

Copy and add the missing apostrophes.

69 six spiders webs _____

70 two girls dresses _____

71 five tigers tails _____

72 nine cows calves _____

73 three mens suits _____

74 four gates hinges _____

75 seven boys towels _____

76 one dogs bone _____

8

Write the **abbreviation** of each of these.

77 centimetre _____   **78** kilogram _____

79 litre _____   **80** millimetre _____

81 square _____   **82** for example _____

83 number _____   **84** that is _____

8

31

Underline the **adjectival phrase** in each sentence.

85 I was pleased when the film, frightening and full of suspense, was over!

86 The morning snow, beautiful but cold, had settled outside my bedroom window.

87 The wild horse, dappled grey with a tangled mane, drank silently at the water's edge.

88 Last night's homework, confusing and difficult, took Nina many hours to complete.

89 Our local swimming pool, green, murky and a little smelly, hadn't been cleaned recently.

90 Ben, strong and athletic, was a capable athlete.

6

These are three ways in which words are derived. Write the appropriate number next to each word to show where you think it came from:

(1) imitating a sound
(2) another language
(3) name of a place or person

91 moo _____   92 cardigan _____

93 autograph _____   94 pizza _____

95 hoover _____   96 whoosh _____

6

Add the missing semicolons to these sentences.

97 Capital punishment no longer takes place in Great Britain it is still used in America.

98 Helen loves doing homework Laura prefers to socialise.

99 We visited the crown jewels jewels indeed fit for a queen.

100 An art gallery in London has a collection of Monet pictures an exhibition which is simply too good to miss.

4

100
TOTAL

Some questions will be answered in the children's own words. Answers to these questions are given in *italics*. Any answers that seem to be in line with these should be marked correct. The use of commas is often subjective. Use the answers given here as guidelines and give full marks if a child has used enough commas to punctuate the sentence sensibly.

Paper 1

1. 1925
2. France
3. 7
4. *60 miles an hour*
5. *a second windscreen in the back*
6. *when you are aged nine, twenty-one seems very old; she was driving so was playing the role of a 'grown-up'*
7. *excited and possibly a little apprehensive*
8. *'Her tone was so confident and cocky it should have scared us to death ...' or 'She had received two full half-hour lessons in driving from the man who delivered the car, and in that enlightened year of 1925 this was considered quite sufficient.'*
9–10. *[answer stating possible events that might have occurred on the drive]*
11. provisions
12. entrance
13. choice
14. advertisement
15. performance
16. bewilderment
17. destruction
18. applause
19. decorator
20. cellar
21. plumber
22. disaster
23. corridor
24. burglar
25. popular
26. circular
27. divisor
28. director
29. proprietor
30. partner
31–35. Dad said that **he was** going to mow the lawn. **He hoped** this **would be** the last time **he would** have to do it this year as **he was** tired of doing it.
36. sceptre
37. scheme
38. scholar
39. school
40. schooner
41–42. They're, their
43–44. their, They're
45–46. There, there
47–48. There, their
49. shouldn't
50. they'll
51. there'll
52. hadn't
53. there's
54. they've
55. I'd
56. won't
57. adjective
58. verb
59. noun
60. adverb
61–63. *[3 compound words each including the word 'light' – e.g. lighthouse, firelight, sunlight]*
64–66. *[3 compound words each including the word 'snow' – e.g. snowdrop, snowfall, snowball]*
67–69. *[3 compound words each including the word 'day' – e.g. daylight, daydream, daytime]*
70. postage
71. sentence
72. parliament
73. machinery
74. fattening
75. mathematics
76. history
77–80. The men were cleaning their houses.
81–82. They jumped over the puddles.
83–86. They bought scarves to support their football teams.
87. thoughts
88. thorns
89. never
90. water
91. work
92. lining
93. basket
94. news
95. speed
96–100. Sam was caught, thank goodness, otherwise I would have been blamed for stealing the sweets, pen, magazine, Harry Potter book and racing car.

Paper 2

1. a dish being thrown
2. no
3. meeting an alien
4. *paranormal means 'beyond normal'*
5. *If science doesn't have an explanation for something it is not 'normal'.*
6. *if they are victims of either a ghost or poltergeist*
7. *[answer stating which area of paranormal activity they find most interesting and why]*
8–9. *[answer stating the difference between their reaction to being aware of a poltergeist and meeting an alien]*
10. mice
11. stories
12. cargoes
13. thieves
14. trolleys
15. potatoes
16. gases

A1

17 oxen
18 roofs
19 valleys
20 3
21 6
22 4
23 7
24 1
25 5
26 2
27–36 cook, crutch, lanyard, wedge, movement, ashore, heaviest, deck, spaces, walk
37 two peas
38 bat
39 cucumber
40 pie
41 gold
42 lead
43 cricket
44 hatter
45 She walked slowly to school today.
46 Ian had a large appetite.
47 Rachel wrote the invitations to her party neatly.
48 She intently watched the TV programme.
49 Softly she sang the lilting tune.
50 They got up early on Sunday.
51–52 He lifted the kitten carefully and put it in the basket.
53 e.g. expand
54 e.g. export
55 e.g. decrease
56 e.g. coarse, thick
57 e.g. free
58 e.g. permanent
59 e.g. inferior
60 e.g. accept, agree
61 e.g. singular
62 e.g. create
63 Does Jess love going swimming?
64 Alice enjoys painting.
65 Bola's coat is in the car.
66 Has Daniel dropped his homework without noticing?
67 They have all received an invitation from Amita.
68 Has Ruben eaten the last cake?
69 crept
70 lost
71 spoke
72 wept
73 threw
74 rang
75 wrote
76 broke
77–83 **They** jumped into the car before **it** sped off at high speed. Joseph whispered that **he** had never seen his mum so cross. **She** reminded **him** of a bull! **They** agreed with **him**.
84–88 "What about the horse**?**" said Thorin. "You don't mention sending that back**.**"
89–91 *[3 words, each with the prefix 'dis' – e.g. disloyal, discontinue, displease]*
92–94 *[3 words, each with the prefix 'mis' – e.g. misunderstand, mislead, misplace]*
95–100
[three interesting sentences using the nouns and verbs provided, including an adjective and adverb in each]

Paper 3

1 evening
2 in a village
3 beside the woods
4–5 *the harness bells; the sound of wind and snow*
6 *because it was cold and dark and there was no farmhouse nearby where they could possibly have food and water*
7 *'The woods are lovely, dark, and deep,'*
8 *[answer stating what they themselves would feel about the woods and why]*
9 *to emphasise how far the traveller still has to go*
10–16 athlete, student, friend, typist, knitter, child, cat
17 north east
18 public limited company
19 please turn over
20 department
21 milligram(s)
22 e.g. Member of Parliament or Military Police or Metropolitan Police
23 e.g. British Summer Time or British Standard Time
24 United Kingdom
25 for
26 in
27 on
28 on
29 for
30 at
31 by
32 up
33 foreign
34 believe
35 achieve
36 conceited
37 neighbour
38 audience
39 height
40 ceiling
41 badly
42 slither
43 quantity
44 woollen
45 where
46 ugly
47 but
48–53 *[the completion of the second clause in six sentences]*
54–55 *[2 words with the root word 'help' – e.g. helpful, helping]*
56–57 *[2 words with the root word 'turn' – e.g. return, returned]*
58–59 *[2 words with the root word 'collect' – e.g. collection, collectable]*
60–61 *[2 words with the root word 'reason' – e.g. reasonable, unreasonable]*

62–63 [2 words with the root word 'agree' – e.g. agreeable, disagree]

64–72 Egyptian, David, February, Wales, Denmark, June, Manchester, Tuesday, Britney [note: queen is an incorrect answer as its capitalisation is dependent on context]

73–74 [2 definitions for the word 'wicked' – e.g. (1) someone or something that is very bad (2) very trendy/really good]

75–76 [2 definitions for the word 'trainer' – e.g. (1) someone who trains someone to do something (2) a type of shoe]

77–78 [2 definitions for the word 'cool' – e.g. (1) fairly cold (2) very trendy]

79–80 [2 definitions for the word 'green' – e.g. (1) a colour (2) environmentally friendly]

81 punishment
82 fragrance
83 arrival
84 length
85 conclusion
86 assistance
87 Gina didn't swim in the sea.
88 There weren't any stars out tonight. or There were no stars out tonight.
89 The dogs didn't wait.
90 The playground wasn't open.
91 Caroline didn't want to/a ride in the car.
92 Raj's family hadn't won any money on the lottery. or Raj's family had won no money on the lottery.

93–100 [eight answers from] you're, you've, won't, they'll, they've, haven't,

they're, you'll, aren't

1 170
2 the avocet
3 they provide havens to keep rare species alive
4 the changing climate
5–6 more frequent sea inundation (of Titchwell) and increasing flooding (of the Ouse Washes)
7 they will become extinct
8–9 e.g. (1) the damage done to species when moving them (2) the expense
10–12 e.g. purr, chug, throb
13–15 e.g. howl, whoosh, whistle
16–18 e.g. plop, gurgle, splash
19 putting
20 talking
21 doing
22 swimming
23 using
24 hiding
25 hoping
26 getting
27 carrying
28 e.g. while, as, because, before, after, and
29 e.g. but
30 e.g. where, and
31 e.g. until, before
32 e.g. as, because, since
33 e.g. because
34 e.g. when, because, and
35 elegant
36 prudent
37 adjacent
38 abundant
39 arrogant
40 extravagant
41 continent
42 immigrant
43 cement
44 e.g. See you later.
45 e.g. You're making fun of me!
46 e.g. I'm not accepting that.
47 e.g. Did you take the day off school?

48 e.g. It was a very good concert.
49 e.g. If you don't come you are boring.
50 e.g. You look good in those sun glasses.
51 The following children are absent today: Amina, Ilesh, Frank, Michael and Fayza.
52 The school magazine reported: No school uniform for a day!
53 An eyewitness stated: The car turned over as it crashed into the tree, just missing three people ...
54 The following classes are out on a school trip today: Class 6L, Class 6T and Class 6M.
55 The local paper reported: School flooded, children sent home.
56–62 piglet, statuette, droplet, owlet, duckling, starlet, majorette
63 the rabbit's food
64 Leanne's hairbrush
65 the players' football
66 the baby's rattle
67 the museum's cafe
68 toddlers' playground
69 bicycle's handlebar
70 Mr Dodd's newspaper
71 author or writer
72 stationery
73 apologised
74 recently or lately
75 present
76 unnecessary or pointless or futile
77–85 [words with the correct number of syllables]
86–100
"I will buy you some new shoes," said Mum, "but not until you have out–grown the ones you are wearing now."
"But these aren't fashionable," complained Sam. "Nobody has shoes like these now."
"You do!" laughed Mum. [or "You do," laughed Mum.]

Paper 5

1. Cairo
2. No
3. second
4. 'solid white fog'; 'you couldn't see twenty yards'
5–6. *scared: e.g. because in the hostile conditions he had to find Jim*
excited: e.g. because of the difficult conditions and the speed he had to work at in order to track down Jim
7. *because he was in some kind of trouble and at night he couldn't be spotted so easily*
8. 'hollering'; 'whooped'
9. *when in fog your senses are confused as you can't see as well, so things can look and sound strange*
10. e.g. recklessly
11. e.g. greedily
12. e.g. brilliantly
13. e.g. vaguely
14. e.g. attentively
15. e.g. neatly
16. e.g. bravely
17. e.g. carefully
18–20. *be good looking, not be nervous, have a good sense of rhythm*
21. *on stage*
22. *phone the Production Office*
23. *a form of test to see who is most suitable for a part in a performance*
24–25. knew, new
26–27. course, coarse
28–29. beech, beach
30–31. practise, practice
32–33. hour, our
34. 3
35. 5
36. 7
37. 6
38. 1
39. 4
40. 2
41. unlock
42. impolite
43. disagree
44. incapable
45. irregular
46. uncover [not discover]
47. disown
48. unreliable
49–51. The mouse lived in the old barn until the child found it.
52–54. The class lined up quietly once its teacher had arrived.
55–59. The satsuma was eaten quickly by the child, who then wanted a chocolate!
60. refresh
61. refugee
62. refund
63. refuse
64. refute
65. regard
66–75. "What time are you going home?" said Jill to her brother. "I don't want to be late."
"I'll go when you are ready," replied Tim.
76–87. *[a clause added to each sentence (one mark) using a different connective each time (one mark)]*
88. salmon
89. wife
90. opportunity
91. half
92. cactus
93. solo
94. canoe
95. puppy
96. blanket
97. torrent of darkness
98. soft cushion
99. cotton wool
100. ribbon of moonlight

Paper 6

1. night
2. deep red
3. 2
4. *it describes the stars twinkling in the sky like jewels*
5. *e.g. because dogs can't speak and in that situation Tim couldn't speak*
6. *money and treasures stolen from some travellers*
7. *one that tells a story*
8–9. *[answer stating how they would have felt and what they would have done if they were Tim]*
10. ran
11. cassette
12. large
13. cried
14. quickly
15. she
16. loveable or lovable
17. useful or useable or usable
18. plentiful
19. wonderful
20. valuable
21. laughable
22. rightful or rightable
23. powerful
24. workable
25–34.

Synonyms	Antonyms
vacant/empty	absence/presence
tranquil/peaceful	here/there
option/choice	coarse/fine
famous/noted	seldom/often
caution/care	few/many

35–42. *[4 sentences, each including a noun and verb from the table and at least one adjective and one adverb of their choice]*
43–49. visitor, worker, editor, relation, adult, pupil, passenger
50–51. One morning, as the sun was rising, Jack crept out of the house.
52. In his hand was a small bag just large enough to carry an apple, two sandwiches and a big slice of cake.
53–54. He turned, looked towards the house, then ran across the field.
55. Jack moved slowly, worried he might be

seen.

56–58 As he entered the cave, his eyes adjusting to the darkness, he recognised the silhouette of Aimee, his young and vulnerable sister.

59 business
60 imaginary
61 conscience
62 environment
63 miscellaneous
64 persuasion
65 stomach
66 necessary
67 possession
68 sequence
69 six spiders' webs
70 two girls' dresses
71 five tigers' tails
72 nine cows' calves
73 three men's suits
74 four gates' hinges
75 seven boys' towels
76 one dog's bone
77 cm
78 kg
79 l
80 mm
81 sq.
82 e.g.
83 no.
84 i.e.
85 I was pleased when the film, <u>frightening and full of suspense</u>, was over!
86 The morning snow, <u>beautiful but cold</u>, had settled outside my bedroom window.
87 The wild horse, <u>dappled grey with a tangled mane</u>, drank silently at the water's edge.
88 Last night's homework, <u>confusing and difficult</u>, took Nina many hours to complete.
89 Our local swimming pool, <u>green, murky and a little smelly</u>, hadn't been cleaned recently.
90 Ben, <u>strong and athletic</u>, was a very capable athlete.
91 1

92 3
93 2
94 2
95 3
96 1
97 Capital punishment no longer takes place in Great Britain; it is still used in America.
98 Helen loves doing homework; Laura prefers to socialise.
99 We visited the crown jewels; jewels indeed fit for a queen.
100 An art gallery in London has a collection of Monet pictures; an exhibition which is simply too good to miss.

Paper 7

1 sausage
2 sugar
3 6
4 *as food is digested in our stomach and intestines it breaks down into substances that are absorbed into the blood and can be used as energy*
5–6 *'fat' contains the most energy and is carried around our body by our blood*
7–8 *we are using more energy than can be supplied by our blood; we could eat foods that supply us with a quick burst of energy*
9 *because after our evening meal most people haven't eaten throughout the night, therefore breakfast is the first meal we can use to top up our energy supplies*
10 7
11 4
12 8
13 9

14 3
15 2
16 5
17 6
18 1
19 The dog's paws
20 The lady's coat
21 The men's work
22 The teachers' cars
23 My cousin's cat
24 The children's umbrellas
25 The woman's bank account
26 The singers' guitars
27 The dentist's chair
28 The flats' walls
29 e.g. hiss
30 e.g. gobble
31 e.g. squeak
32 e.g. neigh
33 e.g. croak
34 e.g. buzz
35 e.g. cluck
36 e.g. howl
37 e.g. over
38 e.g. with
39 e.g. from
40 e.g. along
41 e.g. under
42 e.g. above
43 e.g. by
44 e.g. for
45 lazy
46 happy
47 duty
48 silly
49 heavy
50 hurry
51 beauty
52 tidy
53 gift or perk
54 *they are activities relating to seasonal activities when money is given*
55 *bounty*
56 *they are the looks of people who have already given some of their money away*
57 *innate, a reaction you don't have to think about (an impulse)*
58 *[answer stating how the girls felt seeing the boys enjoying the 'seasonal perks']*

59–69 Saturday, obedience, remain, owners, several, toy, terriers, hounds, judges, animals, prizes

70 is
71 have
72 is
73 are
74 is
75 are
76 Welsh
77 Tibetan
78 Dutch
79 Portuguese

80–92 Jacob called back to the others, "Where are you?" He was beginning to get worried; he hadn't heard them for at least five minutes. "Is that you, Sandy? Please answer if it is."

"Of course it is! Who else would it be?" responded Sandy, giggling.
(or "Of course it is. ...")

93–100
[completion of the table with words with the correct number of syllables]

Paper 8

1 Liverpool FC
2 1892
3 the mess left on the streets
4 *support financially*
5 *they are words usually associated with the game of football*
6 *without the outside influence of the people arriving on match days things would become financially worse for the area*
7 *he thinks his pub won't survive without match days*
8–9 *[answer stating two reasons why a move for Everton FC would be positive]*

10 e.g. adhere
11 e.g. accelerate
12 e.g. abandon or abscond
13 e.g. acute
14 e.g. alter or alteration
15 e.g. abundant
16 e.g. abbreviate or abridge
17 e.g. attempt
18–29

Nouns	Verbs	Adjectives
reality	expect	carefree
uncertainty	caught	happy
energy	drown	foolish
sunlight	met	artificial

30 impatient
31 illegible
32 irresponsible
33 discontented
34 uninformed
35 nonsense
36 inconsiderate
37 uncertain

38–44 As the water trickled off the roof, on to the path and down into the ever increasing stream, Mark wished it would stop raining. Usually a patient boy, he wouldn't have minded being trapped in the club house if he wasn't supposed to have been home ages ago. Mark had left with Tony, Matt, Anil and Rick but had to return as he had forgotten, in all the excitement, his football kit.

45 dynasties
46 surveys
47 frequencies
48 injuries
49 galleries
50 melodies
51 anthologies
52 photocopies
53–55 The young cat, full of fun, killed the mouse; Dad was pleased.
56 The aircraft was nearly empty; empty seats are good for passengers but

bad news for airlines.
57 Polar bears are beginning to move closer to people's homes; it can't be long before there is an attack.
58–60 Rugby training is hard work; we start with a run, continue with 30 press-ups, practise moves and finish with a training match.
61 active
62 active
63 passive
64 passive
65 active
66 active
67 passive
68 active
69–74 *[answers each describing the metaphors]*
75 silently
76 prison
77 dictionary
78 nursery
79 company
80 chocolate
81 different
82 fragrance
83 temperature
84–88 *[answers completing five conditional sentences]*
89 better
90 latest
91 worse
92 least
93–94 harder, cleverer
95–100
[three sentences each with two pronouns]

Paper 9

1 on special occasions
2 three months
3 basin/porringer
4 *to catch any stray splashes of gruel*
5 *They held a meeting.*
6 *he was so miserable and hungry that he would risk anything for some more food*
7 *extreme boldness/*

courage

8 [answer stating what they think happened next]

9 [answer stating how they would have felt watching the scene as one of the other boys]

10 anxious
11 perilous
12 regional
13 choral
14 methodical
15 long
16 ornamental
17 metallic
18 duck's back
19 china shop
20 fiddle
21 March hare or hatter or coot
22 church mouse
23 dodo or doornail
24 sauce
25 altar
26 source
27 practice
28 stationary
29 practise
30 alter
31 desert
32 stationery
33 dessert

34–39 [6 sentences made more interesting by adding a clause to each]

40 has
41 should
42 comes
43 here
44 are
45 will
46 says
47 shall
48 the two cats' tails
49 the five children's coats
50 the ten apples' pips
51 the three dogs' bones
52 the seven houses' keys
53 the nine videos' cases
54 the four horses' foals
55 the six computers' keyboards
56 queen
57 *entrance guarding*
58 *by dancing*
59 *food is near the hive in*

the direction of the sun

60 *every individual bee has an important part in the running of the colony*
61 sophisticated
62 e.g. herd
63 e.g. shoal
64 e.g. troupe or company
65 e.g. plague or swarm
66 e.g. pride
67 e.g. band or group
68 e.g. litter
69 e.g. flock
70 e.g. murder

71–78 engagement, alignment, membership, settlement, ownership, scholarship, hardship, arrangement

79–93 It was **S**unday afternoon and the sun was glinting through the trees. **A**melia called to **G**eorge, "**A**re we going to do something today? **I**'m bored of just sitting here." **A**fter a short pause she called again. **I**t seemed he had decided to hide himself.

94–100

[a mnemonic for each of the listed words]

Paper 10

1 a slave
2 for morning light
3 in Jarnseaxa's hall / Jarnseaxa's island / Jarnseaxa's bed-closet
4 a beautiful Battle-woman

5–7 [three words describing how Elfgift might have felt]

8–9 [in note form, two ideas about how the story might continue]

10–11 <u>censure</u>
 praise
12–13 <u>raise</u>
 lower
14–15 <u>gather</u>
 disperse
16–17 <u>increase</u>
 contract
18–19 <u>minimum</u>

most

20 e.g. whether
21 e.g. until
22 e.g. unless
23 e.g. because
24 e.g. where
25 e.g. or
26 e.g. when
27 rhythm
28 reign
29 knot
30 rhombus
31 column
32 hour
33 hymn
34 guard
35 active
36 passive
37 active
38 active
39 active
40 passive
41 passive
42 3
43 6
44 5
45 2
46 7
47 8
48 1
49 4

50–57 [statements and questions using the words provided]

58–59 far off
 e.g. television

60–61 small or millionth
 e.g. microphone or micrometre

62–63 below or under
 e.g. submerge

64–65 water
 e.g. aquamarine

66–67 self
 e.g. autograph

68 from
69 on
70 to
71 beyond
72 on
73 outside
74 up

75–78 [four sentences, each with a colon]

79 equalise
80 equestrian

81 equilateral
82 equilibrium
83 equinox
84 equipment
85 fought
86 built
87 ran
88 got
89 meant
90 became
91 found
92 felt
93 made
94 understood
95 interesting
96 unfortunately
97 specification
98 infrastructure
99 rehearsal
100 independence

Paper 11

1 1997
2–3 animal welfare, milk production practices
4 *someone who drinks milk or eats dairy products; someone who buys dairy products*
5 *the logo highlights products which meet certain specifications*
6 *a check*
7 *[answer stating whether they think the NDFAS scheme is important and why]*
8–9 *e.g. (1) help sell their product (2) might be expensive to reach the standards set*
10 e.g. boomerang
11 e.g. restaurant
12 e.g. spaghetti
13 e.g. kilt
14 e.g. bungalow
15 e.g. freeway
16 e.g. wok
17 best
18 longest
19 Most
20 tastiest
21 most wonderful
22 least
23 worst
24–29 *[six sentences with an adjectival phrase added to improve each one]*
30 advertiser
31 musician
32 absentee
33 admirer
34 assistant
35 cashier
36 imitator
37 magician
38 teacher
39 competitor
40 went
41 drank
42 threw
43 wore
44 shook
45–46 found, could
47 stole
48 e.g. pop
49 e.g. bang
50 e.g. tick
51 e.g. plop
52 e.g. crack
53 e.g. tinkle
54 e.g. slam
55 e.g. creak
56 e.g. gracefully
57 e.g. attentively
58 e.g. heavily
59 e.g. brightly
60 e.g. stealthily
61 e.g. politely
62 e.g. frequently
63 e.g. fluently
64 e.g. breathlessly
65–72 *[a short argument including the words/phrases in bold, about whether boxing should be banned]*
73 e.g. depression
74 e.g. unhappily
75 e.g. telegraphic
76 e.g. disagreeable
77 e.g. endangered
78 e.g. undivided
79 e.g. subheading
80 e.g. undoing
81–100

As Monty raced off down the beach, Brian and Jess began to feel a little concerned. Monty was a lovely black Labrador who was a little unreliable when it came to listening to commands. "Monty, come back!" called Jess. "We've got to go home." But Monty seemed not to hear. He put his head down to the sand, picked up a scent of something good and was off. "You'd better wait here. I'll chase after him," suggested Brian, beginning to feel annoyed with his lovable dog.

FOOD IS STORED ENERGY

Food contains enormous amounts of energy locked up as chemicals. There is more energy in a single sausage than in a stick of dynamite!

The food that contains the most energy is called **fat**, but substances called **carbohydrates** – found in for example cereals, potatoes and sugar – also contain large amounts of chemical energy.

Where energy is stored

When we digest food, chemical reactions take place in our stomach and our intestines. They break down the food into substances that are absorbed through the walls of the intestine and taken into the blood.

Two of the most common substances in the blood are sugar and fat. Fat is carried by the blood so that it can be used by any of our muscles when we do exercise. Fat is the main source of energy that we need to work all day long.

By contrast, sugar (also carried by the blood) is used for an almost instant source of energy allowing us to move quickly to get out of trouble, or for example, to win a sprint race.

Running out of energy

Sometimes you may feel very tired because you have been exercising hard. This means that you are using up the energy in your muscles and blood faster than more energy can be brought in by the blood supply.

Using up energy

Think of the human body as a machine that needs fuel to carry out its functions. The energy in an apple, for example, will be used up in 30 minutes sleeping or 5 minutes walking.

We measure energy in units called kilojoules. Many foods contain information about their energy content on the packaging labels. Look at some foods and try to compare the energy in a typical serving.

From *Energy: Science in our World* by Brian Knapp

Underline the correct answers.

1   What has more energy, a sausage or a stick of dynamite?
    (sausage, stick of dynamite)

2   Which food energy source do we use if we are being chased?
    (fat, carbohydrates, sugar)

3   How many apples would you need to eat to give you enough energy to walk for
    30 minutes? (1, 3, 6)

3

Answer these questions.

4   In your own words explain how the energy stored in food becomes energy that
    we can use.

    _____

    _____

    _____

5–6   What type of food contains the most energy and how is that energy carried
      around our bodies?

    _____

    _____

    _____

7–8   Why do we sometimes feel tired and what do you think we could do to make us
      feel more alert?

    _____

    _____

    _____

9   Explain why you think for many people 'breakfast is the most important meal of
    the day'.

    _____

    _____

6

Match the following proverbs/expressions with their meanings. Write the correct number in the space.

10	to call a spade a spade	_____	(1) to begin to understand
11	to bury the hatchet	_____	(2) back to work
12	by hook or by crook	_____	(3) not to take sides – to remain neutral
13	a bolt from the blue	_____	(4) to forget past quarrels
14	to sit on the fence	_____	(5) neat and tidy
15	back in harness	_____	(6) to change for the better
16	spick and span	_____	(7) to be very outspoken
17	to turn over a new leaf	_____	(8) by any means
18	to see daylight	_____	(9) something unexpected

9

Write the possessive form of each of these phrases, i.e. with an apostrophe.

Example   The funnels of the ships   _The ships' funnels_

19 The paws of the dog   _____

20 The coat of the lady   _____

21 The work of the men   _____

22 The cars of the teachers   _____

23 The cat of my cousin   _____

24 The umbrellas of the children   _____

25 The bank account of the woman   _____

26 The guitars of the singers   _____

27 The chair of the dentist   _____

28 The walls of the flats   _____

10

Write an **onomatopoeic** word associated with each of the following animals.

29	snake	_____	**30**	turkey	_____
31	mouse	_____	**32**	horse	_____
33	frog	_____	**34**	bee	_____
35	chicken	_____	**36**	wolf	_____

8

Complete the following sentences by writing a **preposition** in each space.

37 He climbed _____ the gate with ease.

38 Mark corresponds _____ two penfriends.

39 Granny is suffering _____ arthritis.

40 We walked slowly _____ the river bank.

41 Her paper was hidden _____ the pile of books.

42 Keep your head _____ the water when learning to swim.

43 I put it _____ the radiator.

44 We waited _____ the bus.

8

Write the root of each of the words.

45 laziness _____   **46** happiness _____

47 dutiful _____   **48** silliness _____

49 heavily _____   **50** hurried _____

51 beautiful _____   **52** tidily _____

8

The week before Christmas, when the snow seemed to lie thickest, was the moment for carol-singing; and when I think back to those nights it is to the crunch of snow and to the lights of the lanterns on it. Carol-singing in my village was a special tithe for the boys; the girls had little to do with it. Like haymaking, blackberrying, stone-clearing, and wishing-people-a-happy-Easter, it was one of our seasonal perks.

    By instinct we knew just when to begin it; a day too soon and we should have been unwelcome, a day too late and we should have received lean looks from people whose bounty was already exhausted. When the true moment came, exactly balanced, we recognised it and were ready ...

From *Cider with Rosie* by Laurie Lee

Answer these questions.

53 A tithe used to be a tax. What do you think it means in this extract?

_____

54 Why are the activities listed seen as 'seasonal perks'?

_____

55 Which word means generosity?

_____

56 Why does Laurie Lee describe the faces of people as having 'lean looks' if they arrived a day too late?

_____

_____

57 What does 'instinct' mean?

_____

58 How do you think the girls felt, being unable to do the same activities as the boys?

_____

_____

_____

6

In the following passage there are blanks. The jumbled word in brackets, when the letters are rearranged, makes a word to fill the blank.

59–69 Last _____ **(aaurstdy)** my friend and I went to a Dog Show.

First we saw the _____ **(obcdeeein)** Class. The dogs had to

_____ **(narmei)** where they were, even though their _____

(swoner) had walked away. There were _____ **(verseal)** other

classes. One was for _____ **(oyt)** dogs, another was for

_____ **(trrreeis)** and a third was for _____ **(hsunod)**. The

_____ **(jusdeg)** looked carefully at the _____ **(slamina)** before

awarding the _____ **(pzesir)**.

11

Underline the correct word in the brackets.

70 Not one of the children (are, is) allowed in the sea.

71 All of you but one (have, has) brothers.

72 Neither of the children (are, is) from this town.

73 All the children (are, is) having a hamburger.

74 Which one of you three (are, is) going to do it?

75 How many of you (are, is) eleven years old?

6

Fill each blank with an **adjective** based on the name of a country.

76 _____ lamb comes from Wales.

77 _____ rugs are made in Tibet.

78 Holland is the home of the _____ people.

79 _____ people come from Portugal.

4

Copy and punctuate the passage correctly.

80–92 Jacob called back to the others Where are you He was beginning to get worried he hadn't heard them for at least five minutes Is that you Sandy Please answer if it is

Of course it is Who else would it be responded Sandy giggling

13

Complete the table.

93–100

No. of syllables	Word		
3			
4			
5	*dissatisfaction*		

8

100
TOTAL

GROUNDS FOR CONCERN
THE FINAL WHISTLE

Everton FC is the latest club to have grown too big for its working-class boots and is moving out of the area to a state-of-the-art stadium. So what happens to the people and communities that are left behind?

What happens to the inner city when a football club that dominates its terrace streets, helps sustain its corner shops, cafes and pubs – and crucially, gives the area a lift and an identity – ups sticks and moves across or out of town to a shiny new stadium? Growing numbers of cities are finding out as their famous clubs, embedded for decades in low-income areas, abandon their windy stands, comfortless bars and insanitary toilets for glitzier surroundings.

There is an air of gloom in north Liverpool where Everton is planning to abandon the Walton area and Liverpool FC, too, is contemplating a move. Walton MP Peter Kilfoyle is among those who fear it will be disastrous if both clubs leave. "It is already an extremely depressed area right at the heart of the biggest poverty cluster in the country," he says. "It is essential that at least one club stays, because otherwise the community is socially excluded."

The Everton club has been based in Walton since 1878, although it did not move to the patch of wasteland that became the Goodison Park stadium until August 1892. The club is now planning to move to a £125m stadium on Liverpool's waterfront in time for the 2006 season.

Everton has a complex relationship with the local community: some residents grumble about match-day litter and traffic congestion, but few want it to leave. The club is woven into the social, economic – even spiritual – fabric of the area – and it has been there for so long that no one can visualise what life will be like without it on the door-step.

Small businesses nearby are bracing themselves to be hard hit. Walton is a place where a pensioner can get a haircut for £3 and where almost every second shop is a discount store. Jim Kennedy, landlord of the Netley pub – one of the few in the area still flourishing – does not relish the prospect of what will happen. "It will kill the area," he says bluntly. "The only reason we survive is because of match days. It is not surprising that every pub around here is up for sale. There are too many pubs in this area.

"On match days we are packed with people meeting up before they go to the game. It's like a tradition for them."

From *The Guardian Society* Wednesday, October 24, 2001

Underline the correct answers.

1. Everton FC is planning to move to a new stadium by the year 2006. What other football club in the area is contemplating a change?
   (Everton United, Liverpool FC, Manchester City)

2. Since when has Everton FC been based at Goodison Park?
   (1878, 1892, 1896)

3. Why do some residents grumble about match days?
   (the mess left on the streets, the noise, the shops being busy)

Answer these questions.

4. In the first paragraph the word 'sustain' has been used. Explain what it means here.

   _____

5. Why do you think the reporter has titled this article 'Grounds for concern – The final whistle'?

   _____

   _____

   _____

6. Why does Peter Kilfoyle MP think the possible football club moves could be disastrous?

   _____

   _____

   _____

7. Why is Jim Kennedy particularly concerned about Everton FC moving stadium?

   _____

   _____

   _____

3

8–9 Write two reasons why you think changing stadiums would be a positive move for Everton FC.

(1) _____

_____

_____

(2) _____

_____

_____

6

Write a word, beginning with *a*, which has the same meaning as the word on the left.

10	stick	ad_____	**11**	quicken	ac_____
12	leave	ab_____	**13**	sharp	ac_____
14	change	al_____	**15**	plentiful	ab_____
16	shorten	ab_____	**17**	try	at_____

8

Put these words in the correct columns.

18–29

happy	energy	expect	caught	met
uncertainty	drown	foolish	sunlight	reality
carefree	artificial			

Nouns	Verbs	Adjectives

12

Write an **antonym** for each word by adding a **prefix**.

30	patient	_____	**31**	legible	_____
32	responsible	_____	**33**	contented	_____
34	informed	_____	**35**	sense	_____
36	considerate	_____	**37**	certain	_____

8

Add the missing commas to the passage.

38–44 As the water trickled off the roof on to the path and down into the ever increasing stream Mark wished it would stop raining. Usually a patient boy he wouldn't have minded being trapped in the club house if he wasn't supposed to have been home ages ago. Mark had left with Tony Matt Anil and Rick but had to return as he had forgotten in all the excitement his football kit.

7

Write the **plural** form of each of these words.

45	dynasty	_____	**46** survey	_____
47	frequency	_____	**48** injury	_____
49	gallery	_____	**50** melody	_____
51	anthology	_____	**52** photocopy	_____

8

Add the missing semicolons and commas to these sentences.

53–55 The young cat full of fun killed the mouse Dad was pleased.

56 The aircraft was nearly empty empty seats are good for passengers but bad news for airlines.

57 Polar bears are beginning to move closer to people's homes it can't be long before there is an attack.

58–60 Rugby training is hard work we start with a run continue with 30 press-ups practise moves and finish with a training match.

8

State whether each of these sentences has an **active** or **passive verb**.

61 Brian washed the dishes. _____

62 Janie wrote her diary. _____

63 The mouse was chased by the cat. _____

64 The cyclist was struck by the lorry. _____

65 Jeremy poured the water into a bucket. _____

66 Columbus reached America in 1492. _____

67 The moon was first visited by Neil Armstrong. _____

68 The dog bit my arm. _____

8

Explain what each of these **metaphors** means.

69 The sky was on fire.

_____

70 The moon was a ghostly galleon.

_____

71 The birds were a joyful choir.

_____

72 The thunder is an angry giant.

_____

73 The clouds were cotton wool.

_____

74 The sea was an angry dog.

_____

`6`

Circle the unstressed vowels.

75	silently	**76**	prison	**77**	dictionary
78	nursery	**79**	company	**80**	chocolate
81	different	**82**	fragrance	**83**	temperature

`9`

Complete each of these **conditional** sentences.

84 Sundeep will go to the shop _____

85 The battery in your mobile phone will run out _____

_____

86 We might go to the cinema_____

_____

87 Gran will take the cake out the oven _____

88 We will go by train _____

_____

`5`

Underline the correct word in brackets.

89   Has Keith or Kim the (good, better, best) bat?

90   Of all the children he was the (late, later, latest) to arrive.

91   The more sweets you eat the (bad, worse, worst) your teeth will be.

92   The (little, less, least) you can expect is to receive a letter.

93–94   The (hard, harder, hardest) you work the (clever, cleverer, cleverest) you will be.

`6`

Write three sentences, each including two **pronouns**.

95–96   _____

_____

97–98   _____

_____

99–100   _____

_____

`6`

`100`
TOTAL

Paper 9

The room in which the boys were fed, was a large stone hall, with a copper at one end: out of which the master, dressed in an apron for the purpose, and assisted by one or two women, ladled the gruel at meal-times. Of this festive composition each boy had one porringer, and no more – except on occasions of great public rejoicing, when he had two ounces and a quarter of bread besides. The bowls never wanted washing. The boys polished them with their spoons till they shone again; and when they had performed this operation (which never took very long, the spoons being nearly as large as the bowls), they would sit staring at the copper, with such eager eyes, as if they could have devoured the very bricks of which it was composed; employing themselves, meanwhile, in sucking their fingers most assiduously, with the view of catching up any stray splashes of gruel that might have been cast thereon. Boys have generally excellent appetites. Oliver Twist and his companions suffered the tortures of slow starvation for three months: at last they got so voracious and wild with hunger, that one boy, who was tall for his age, and hadn't been used to that sort of thing (for his father had kept a small cookshop), hinted darkly to his companions, that unless he had another basin of gruel *per diem,* he was afraid he might some night happen to eat the boy who slept next to him, who happened to be a weakly youth of tender age. He had a wild, hungry eye; and they implicitly believed him. A council was held; lots were cast who should walk up to the master after supper that evening, and ask for more; and it fell to Oliver Twist.

The evening arrived; the boys took their places. The master, in his cook's uniform, stationed himself at the copper; his pauper assistants ranged themselves behind him; the gruel was served out; and a long grace was said over the short commons. The gruel disappeared; the boys whispered to each other, and winked at Oliver; while his next neighbours nudged him. Child as he was, he was desperate with hunger, and reckless with misery. He rose from the table; and advancing to the master, basin and spoon in hand, said: somewhat alarmed at his own temerity:

'Please, sir, I want some more.'

The master was a fat, healthy man; but he turned very pale. He gazed in stupefied astonishment on the small rebel for some seconds, and then clung for support to the copper. The assistants were paralysed with wonder; the boys with fear.

'What!' said the master at length, in a faint voice.

'Please, sir,' replied Oliver, 'I want some more.'

From *Oliver Twist* by Charles Dickens

Underline the correct answers.

1 When were the boys given bread?
   (on special occasions, every day, never)

2 For how long had the boys been starving?
   (a week, three months, a year)

2

Answer these questions.

3 Find another word in the passage for 'a bowl'.

_____

4 Why did the boys suck their fingers?

_____

_____

5 Write in your own words 'A council was held'.

_____

6 Oliver is described as 'reckless with misery'. What does this mean?

_____

_____

_____

45

7 Write a definition for the word 'temerity'.

_____

8 What do you think happened immediately after Oliver had said 'Please sir, I want some more'?

_____

_____

9 Imagine you are one of the boys in the room watching Oliver walk up to the master. What thoughts were going through your mind?

_____

_____

_____

7

From each of the words in bold make an **adjective** to fit the sentence.

10 **anxiety**   The _____ woman waited for his return.

11 **peril**   The mountaineers set out on their _____ climb.

12 **region**   They heard the report on the _____ news.

13 **choir**   The _____ society performed at the concert.

14 **method**   They tackled the task in a very _____ way.

15 **length**   Her _____ dress was much admired.

16 **ornament**   The _____ gate was painted white.

17 **metal**   It made a _____ noise when it fell to the ground.

8

Complete these **similes**.

18 Like water off a _____.

19 Like a bull in a _____.

20 As fit as a _____.

21 As mad as a _____.

22 As poor as a _____.

23 As dead as a _____.

6

Use the words in bold to fill the gaps.

sauce	practice	desert	alter	stationary
source	practise	dessert	altar	stationery

24   We all like apple _____ with pork.

25   There were beautiful lilies on the _____ .

26   The _____ of the River Dee is in North Wales.

27   I must do some _____ .

28   The train was _____ ; they need not have hurried.

29   The team must _____ their bowling.

30   Miss Bell must _____ her timetable.

31   The Sahara _____ is in Africa.

32   "You will need more _____ to write all those letters."

33   We had peaches and cream for our _____ .

10

Make the sentences more interesting by adding a **clause** to each of them.

34   My friend knows more about horses than I do.

_____

_____

35   My Uncle Matt is coming to stay.

_____

_____

36   We enjoyed the band at the wedding.

_____

_____

37   Harry swam thirty-six lengths of the school pool.

_____

_____

38 I love going out on my bike.

_____

_____

39 This year we are going on holiday to France.

_____

_____

6

Write the modern version of each of the following words.

40	hath	_____	**41**	shouldst	_____	
42	cometh	_____	**43**	hither	_____	
44	art	_____	**45**	wilt	_____	
46	saith	_____	**47**	shalt	_____	

8

Add the missing apostrophes.

48 the two cats tails   **49** the five childrens coats

50 the ten apples pips   **51** the three dogs bones

52 the seven houses keys   **53** the nine videos cases

54 the four horses foals   **55** the six computers keyboards

8

A bee colony is a family community of which every individual is an integral part. The life of the honey bee colony is potentially endless; the continued survival of the colony results from the fact that young queens replace the old. The degree of social organisation in the colony is most evident in the division of labour. Tasks are assigned according to age. After performing tasks within the hive (such as cleaning, brood nursing and comb building) a worker bee becomes, after about twenty days, an entrance guard, and finally a collector, remaining at this job until her death.

The highly integrated activities of the colony require sophisticated methods of passing information among its members. The dance of the honey bee is perhaps the most remarkable. After a bee has discovered a new source of food, she tells other bees about it by means of various dance-like movements. If the food source is near a hive, a 'round' dance is performed. A 'tail-wagging' dance indicates that the food source is more than 80 metres away. An upward tail-wagging run means, 'the flight is towards the sun'.

From Did you know? Fascinating facts from Encyclopaedia Britannica

56 What name is given to the bee in charge of the colony?

_____

57 What do the middle-aged bees do?

_____

58 How do bees send messages?

_____

59 If a bee danced a round dance with an upward tail-wagging run, where would the food source be found?

_____

60 Describe what is meant by 'every individual is an integral part'.

_____

_____

61 Find a word in the extract that means 'complicated'.

_____

6

Add the missing **collective nouns**.

62 A _____ of cattle.

63 A _____ of herring.

64 A _____ of dancers.

65 A _____ of insects.

66 A _____ of lions.

67 A _____ of musicians.

68 A _____ of puppies.

69 A _____ of sheep.

70 A _____ of crows.

9

Add the **suffix** *ship* or *ment* to each of these words.

71–78   engage   align   member   settle   owner

                         scholar   hard   arrange

_____   _____   _____

_____   _____   _____

_____   _____

8

Rewrite the passage, separating the words correctly and adding the missing capital letters and punctuation.

79–93   itwassundayafternoonandthesunwasglintingthroughthetreesameliacalledto georgearewegoingtodosomethingtodayi'mboredofjustsittinghereafterashort pauseshecalledagainitseemedhehaddecidedtohidehimself

_____

_____

_____

_____

_____

_____

15

Make up your own **mnemonic** for each of these words.

94   separate   _____

95   argument   _____

96   continuous   _____

97   weight   _____

98   concentration   _____

99   permanent   _____

100   unfortunately   _____

7

100
TOTAL

Paper 10

Elfgift was woken by cold, and by the flat, harsh cry of a crow. He sat, and found himself in the open air, in the cold grey dusk of early morning. He looked about, but the dark shape of Jarnseaxa's hall was not there, nor the dark shapes of familiar trees. Nor was the sound of the wind in the trees the sound he had grown used to; nor was there the sound of the sea around Jarnseaxa's island. The crow croaked again.

He got to his feet, and found that he was dressed in a limp tunic of homespun wool, grown soft by much use; and that he was barelegged and barefoot, like a slave. It was cold. He hugged himself, and rubbed the cold toes of one foot against the other calf.

His weapons and armour were gone. He hadn't even a knife. He poked about in the leaf-mould where he had been lying, and found nothing – not a flask, not a loaf, not a leather cloak to keep the rain off.

He waited, shivering, until the dusk lightened, and then explored a little, but still it was so hard to see in the dim light under the trees that only the quickness Jarnseaxa had taught him kept him from bashing his head on branches and blundering into thorn thickets.

He was in a strange forest. Not one tree, not one path did he know. He stopped at a brown stream, where foxgloves leaned over the water, drank, and tried to remember how he had come there. But he could only remember falling asleep beside Jarnseaxa, with his arms around her, in the warmth of the bed-closet.

As the daylight strengthened, and showed him the many trees, with their litter of leaves and fallen branches around them, the tangles of low bushes, the stumps eaten by fungi and strewn round with rotten wood; as cold water dripped on him, and his bare feet floundered in cold, slippery leaf-litter, then, as he shivered, he began to ask himself: Had there ever been a beautiful Battle-woman and a warm bed? Or had that been the dream of a hungry slave?

From *Elfgift* by Susan Price

Underline the correct answers.

1 What was Elfgift dressed like?
(a soldier, an elf, a slave)

2 Why did Elfgift wait before he explored his surroundings?
(to get warm, for Jarnseaxa, for morning light)

Answer these questions.

3 Where had Elfgift expected to wake up?

_____

_____

4 Who was Jarnseaxa?

_____

5–7   Write three words that describe how Elfgift might have felt.

_____   _____   _____

8–9   In note form write two ideas about how you think this story might continue.

(1) _____

_____

_____

_____

(2) _____

_____

_____

_____

7

Underline the word on each line which has the same meaning as the word in bold, and ring the word which has the opposite meaning.

10–11	**blame**	wrong	careless	censure	bad	praise
12–13	**elevate**	high	raise	lower	elude	bottom
14–15	**assemble**	disperse	divide	together	unite	gather
16–17	**expand**	larger	contract	smaller	increase	disband
18–19	**least**	little	most	minimum	lot	more

10

Add a different **conjunction** to complete each sentence.

20   I intend to go _____ you like it or not.

21   We had to wait in the rain _____ the bus came.

22   You won't finish your drawing _____ you hurry up.

23   You must make the cake _____ it is your party.

24   They went to Switzerland _____ there was plenty of snow.

25   Will you come for a walk _____ do you want to watch television?

26   The playground will be much better _____ it is resurfaced.

7

Each of these words has a missing silent letter. Rewrite each word with its missing letter.

27 rythm _____   28 rein _____

29 not _____   30 rombus _____

31 colum _____   32 our _____

33 hym _____   34 gard _____

State whether each of these sentences has an **active** or **passive verb**.

35 The dog eats his bone. _____

36 The ice-cream will be eaten by Grandad. _____

37 Jess swam thirty lengths of the pool. _____

38 The car crashed into the lamp post. _____

39 Rudi caught the thief. _____

40 The bill will be paid by Uncle Rick. _____

41 Alice was taken to the cinema by her parents. _____

Match each word with its **definition** in bold by writing the correct number in the space.

(1) **hermit**   (2) **moisture**   (3) **frighten**   (4) **nearby**

(5) **dregs**   (6) **sitting**   (7) **enemy**   (8) **responsible**

42 intimidate _____   43 sedentary _____

44 sediment _____   45 humidity _____

46 adversary _____   47 liable _____

48 recluse _____   49 adjacent _____

Write a statement and a question that include the words in bold.

50–51 **Peter   homework**

Statement _____

Question _____

52–53 **sailing   France   holiday**

Statement _____

Question _____

54–55 **photograph class yesterday**

Statement _____

Question _____

56–57 **chickenpox bed infectious**

Statement _____

Question _____

Write what you think each **prefix** means and then write a word with each prefix.

e.g. **bi =**   *two*   *bicycle*

58–59 **tele =** _____   _____

60–61 **micro =** _____   _____

62–63 **sub =** _____   _____

64–65 **aqua =** _____   _____

66–67 **auto =** _____   _____

Underline the **prepositions** in the following sentences.

68 His book is different from mine.

69 Mrs Trueman is an authority on beetles.

70 That is an exception to the rule.

71 They were not allowed beyond the fence.

72 The drink spilt on the table.

73 Susie saw the strange man outside her window.

74 The fireman raced up the ladder to save the child.

Write four sentences, each with a colon. In two sentences use the colon to introduce a quotation and in the other two to introduce a list.

75 _____

_____

_____

76 _____

_____

_____

77 _____

_____

_____

78 _____

_____

_____

4

Put these words in **alphabetical order**.

equilibrium	**equipment**	**equilateral**
equalise	**equinox**	**equestrian**

79 (1) _____ **80** (2) _____ **81** (3) _____

82 (4) _____ **83** (5) _____ **84** (6) _____

6

Write the simple **past tense** of these **verbs**.

85 to fight _____ **86** to build _____

87 to run _____ **88** to get _____

89 to mean _____ **90** to become _____

91 to find _____ **92** to feel _____

93 to make _____ **94** to understand _____

10

Rewrite these words correctly.

95 intresting _____ **96** unfortuntely _____

97 specfication _____ **98** infrstructure _____

99 rehersal _____ **100** indepndence _____

6

100 TOTAL

Paper 11

National Dairy Farm Assured Scheme (NDFAS)
Benefits of the NDFAS

A Scheme Developed by the Industry

In 1997 the committee for the National Dairy Farm Assured Scheme was established. It comprised representatives from key sectors of the dairy industry who now form the Board of NDFAS Ltd.

The committee developed a set of standards that addressed both animal welfare and milk production practices in an attempt to provide consumers with greater confidence and further reassurance about the quality of milk and dairy products that they buy.

Why should consumers be interested in the National Dairy Farm Assured Scheme?

The 'Little Red Tractor'

The Board of the NDFAS has taken the decision to join Assured Food Standards and now having met all of the qualifying criteria for this initiative have achieved full membership. Milk and dairy products produced by NDFAS registered milk purchasers can now bear the 'British Farm Standard' logo.

The British Farm Standard is a mark of real quality – only products that have been produced to the highest specification are eligible to use the logo.

BRITISH FARM STANDARD

Credibility

This new scheme currently represents more than 80% of active GB dairy farmers through milk purchaser membership of the Scheme.

Besides having the backing of the major supermarkets, the Scheme also offers producers the option of approval for assurance to the NDFAS standards simultaneously with accreditation to the RSPCA's welfare labelling scheme, Freedom Food, via the one inspection.

Standards

The farm assessment standards of the National Scheme set a benchmark for consistent standards across milk purchasers who have registered with the NDFAS.

How will the Scheme help to ensure that a quality product (which considers animal welfare and the environment as well as milk hygiene and quality) will be delivered?

This will be achieved through the following:
- Carrying out regular audits of milk purchaser members.
- Carrying out random auditing of farms.

From *National Dairy Farm Assured Scheme – Benefits of the NDFAS* leaflet

Underline the correct answers.

1   When was the NDFAS committee established?
    (1979, 1997, 1999)

2–3   What do the NDFAS standards address?
    (consumer confidence, animal welfare, the quality of dairy products, milk production practices)

3

Answer these questions.

4   What is a 'consumer' of milk and dairy products?

5   According to the leaflet, why is it a good thing that a large percentage of milk and dairy products now show the British Farm Standard logo?

6   Explain in your own words what an 'audit' is.

7   Do you think the NDFAS scheme is important? Explain your answer.

8–9 Write two views a farmer might have of the NDFAS scheme.

(1) _____

_____

(2) _____

6

_____

Write a word that you think originated in each of these countries.

10 Australia _____

11 France _____

12 Italy _____

13 Scotland _____

14 India _____

7

15 America _____

16 China _____

In each space, write the superlative form of the word in bold.

17 **good** This is the _____ party I have ever been to.

18 **long** The _____ road is in the Pennines.

19 **many** _____ of you have brought your wellingtons.

20 **tasty** Your mince pies are the _____ I have ever had.

21 **wonderful** It was quite the _____ place I have ever visited.

22 **little** Be very quiet! Make the _____ noise possible.

23 **bad** It was the _____ storm for many years.

7

Copy these sentences, adding an **adjectival phrase** to improve each one.

24 Mr Trump chased the children out of his garden.

_____

25 The school netball team won the cup.

_____

26 The dogs ran towards the sheep.

_____

27 The baby loved having a bath.

_____

28 The Walker family watched the sun set over the hill.

_____

29 George's sailing boat capsized in the sea.

_____

| | 6 |

Write the name of the person who 'fits' the word on the left.

e.g. consult *consultant*

30	advertise	_____	**31**	music	_____
32	absent	_____	**33**	admire	_____
34	assist	_____	**35**	cash	_____
36	imitate	_____	**37**	magic	_____
38	teach	_____	**39**	compete	_____

| | 10 |

Write the **verb** in each sentence in its **past tense**.

40 Today we go to the museum.

Yesterday we _____ to the museum.

41 We drink milk with our tea.

We _____ milk with our tea.

42 They throw the ball over the wall.

They _____ the ball over the wall.

43 I wear my new jeans today.

I _____ my new jeans today.

44 Tom shakes the trees to make the apples drop.

Tom _____ the trees to make the apples drop.

45–46 I find that I can do it.

I _____ that I _____ do it.

47 The dogs steal the meat.

The dogs _____ the meat.

Write an **onomatopoeic** word for each object.

48	cork	_____	**49**	drum	_____	
50	clock	_____	**51**	water	_____	
52	whip	_____	**53**	coins	_____	
54	door	_____	**55**	stairs	_____	

Write an **adverb** that describes the **verb**.

56 The ballerina danced _____ .

57 The class listened _____ .

58 The rain beat _____ .

59 The sun shone _____ .

60 The burglar crept _____ .

61 The child answered _____ .

62 The boy coughed _____ .

63 The actress spoke _____ .

64 The athlete finished _____ .

Write a short argument, including the words/phrases in bold, that explains your opinions about whether boxing should be banned.

65–72

viewpoint	**conclusion**	**opinion**
furthermore	**as well as**	**believe**
contention	**although**	

_____

_____

_____

_____

_____

_____

_____

_____

_____

_____

8

Add a **prefix** and a **suffix** to each of these **root words** to make one new word.

73 press _____   **74** happy _____

75 graph _____   **76** agree _____

77 danger _____   **78** divide _____

79 head _____   **80** do _____

8

Copy this passage, adding the missing punctuation.

81–100 As Monty raced off down the beach Brian and Jess began to feel a little concerned Monty was a lovely black Labrador who was a little unreliable when it came to listening to commands Monty come back called Jess Weve got to go home But Monty seemed not to hear He put his head down to the sand picked up a scent of something good and was off

Youd better wait here Ill chase after him suggested Brian beginning to feel annoyed with his lovable dog

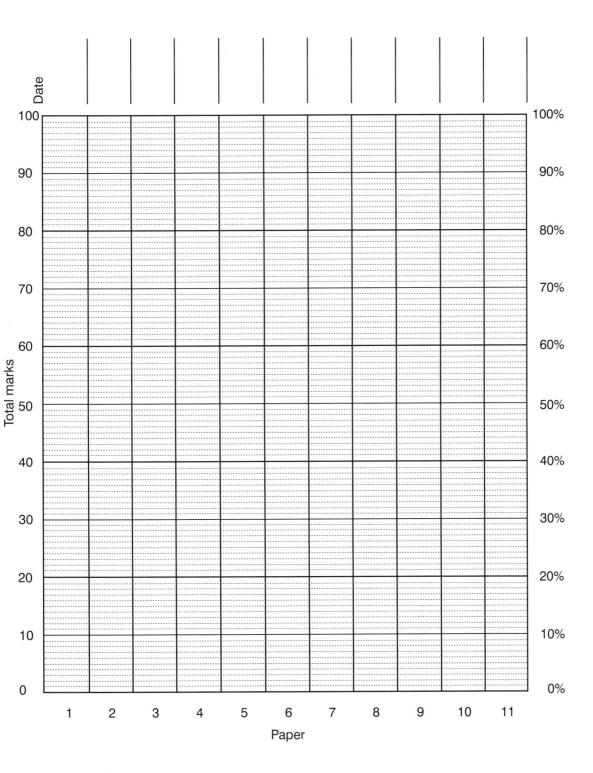